EMMANUEL JOSEPH

Daily Anchors, Small Habits to Ground Your Focus, Calm Your Mind, and Strengthen Ties

Copyright © 2025 by Emmanuel Joseph

All rights reserved. No part of this publication may be reproduced, stored or transmitted in any form or by any means, electronic, mechanical, photocopying, recording, scanning, or otherwise without written permission from the publisher. It is illegal to copy this book, post it to a website, or distribute it by any other means without permission.

First edition

This book was professionally typeset on Reedsy.
Find out more at reedsy.com

Contents

1. Chapter 1: The Power of Morning Rituals — 1
2. Chapter 2: Breathing Techniques for Immediate Calm — 3
3. Chapter 3: Mindful Eating for Improved Focus — 5
4. Chapter 4: The Art of Journaling for Self-Reflection — 7
5. Chapter 5: Evening Rituals for Restful Sleep — 9
6. Chapter 6: The Impact of Gratitude Practices — 11
7. Chapter 7: The Benefits of Physical Movement — 13
8. Chapter 8: Digital Detox for Mental Clarity — 15
9. Chapter 9: Acts of Kindness for Emotional Fulfillment — 17
10. Chapter 10: Creative Expression for Emotional Release — 19
11. Chapter 11: Mindful Communication for Stronger Connections — 21
12. Chapter 12: Decluttering for Mental Space — 23
13. Chapter 13: Nature Connection for Grounding — 25
14. Chapter 14: Financial Mindfulness for Stability — 27
15. Chapter 15: Mindful Consumption for Sustainability — 29
16. Chapter 16: Meditation for Mental Clarity — 31
17. Chapter 17: The Journey of Personal Growth — 32

1

Chapter 1: The Power of Morning Rituals

Starting each day with a consistent morning routine sets the tone for everything that follows. Small actions like making your bed, stretching, or savoring your first cup of coffee can ground you in the present moment, creating a sense of calm and readiness. These seemingly mundane activities help build momentum, laying the foundation for a more focused and productive day. By crafting a morning ritual that resonates with you, you signal to yourself that you prioritize self-care and intentionality.

Beyond productivity, morning rituals can serve as anchors for mental wellbeing. As the world swirls around us, having a set of actions to return to can be incredibly stabilizing. It creates a small oasis of predictability and control amidst life's uncertainties. Connecting with yourself first thing can also enhance mindfulness, helping you approach the day's challenges with a clearer, more centered perspective.

Morning rituals can extend into nurturing relationships as well. Shared routines, like enjoying breakfast together or taking a morning walk with loved ones, foster a sense of community and connection. These moments can be opportunities for meaningful conversations and shared experiences, reinforcing the bonds between family and friends. By committing to these small habits, you're not just grounding yourself, but also strengthening the ties that bind you to others.

Reflecting on the origins and impact of morning rituals, it's clear that their simplicity belies profound benefits. Historically, various cultures have valued the sanctity of the morning, recognizing it as a time for spiritual and physical rejuvenation. Adopting and personalizing these practices can transform mornings from a rushed, chaotic start to a serene and empowering beginning.

2

Chapter 2: Breathing Techniques for Immediate Calm

In the hustle and bustle of daily life, it's easy to get overwhelmed. One of the most accessible tools for regaining composure is the power of breath. Deep breathing techniques can serve as quick resets, allowing you to re-center and calm your mind no matter the circumstances. By consciously controlling your breath, you engage your parasympathetic nervous system, which helps counteract stress responses.

The simplicity of breathing exercises makes them highly effective and versatile. Techniques like box breathing, where you inhale for a count of four, hold for four, exhale for four, and hold again for four, can be practiced anywhere. This rhythmic pattern calms the mind and reduces anxiety. Other methods, such as diaphragmatic breathing or alternate nostril breathing, can be tailored to specific needs, offering immediate relief.

Incorporating these techniques into your daily routine can lead to cumulative benefits. Regular practice can improve overall respiratory function, increase mindfulness, and promote a sense of physical and emotional balance. These habits create a bridge between mind and body, enhancing self-awareness and resilience in the face of stress.

Breathing exercises also hold potential for strengthening interpersonal relationships. When shared, these techniques can become communal practices that foster connection and mutual support. Whether it's a group meditation session or a simple moment of collective calm, breathing together can unite individuals, creating a shared sense of tranquility and understanding.

3

Chapter 3: Mindful Eating for Improved Focus

Eating is a daily activity that often goes unnoticed in its potential to ground us. Mindful eating transforms meals from routine consumption into meaningful experiences. By paying attention to each bite, savoring flavors, and acknowledging the nourishment your food provides, you create a deeper connection with yourself and your body. This practice can enhance focus and presence, turning mealtime into a deliberate act of self-care.

Mindful eating begins with preparation. Engaging in the process of selecting, cooking, and presenting food with intention can be a meditative experience. The act of preparing a meal becomes an exercise in mindfulness, allowing you to immerse yourself in the sensory details and rhythms of cooking. This level of engagement cultivates a sense of appreciation and mindfulness that carries over into the act of eating.

As you eat mindfully, you develop a greater awareness of hunger and satiety cues, leading to healthier eating habits. By slowing down and truly experiencing your food, you create space for reflection and gratitude. This heightened awareness can extend beyond meals, positively influencing other aspects of your life by fostering a mindset of intentional living.

Mindful eating can also be a powerful tool for strengthening relationships.

Sharing meals with loved ones, while practicing mindful eating, can create opportunities for deeper connection and conversation. The act of eating together, with full presence and appreciation, becomes a shared ritual that reinforces communal bonds and fosters mutual understanding.

4

Chapter 4: The Art of Journaling for Self-Reflection

Journaling is a simple yet profound habit that can serve as an anchor for self-reflection and emotional clarity. By dedicating time each day to write down your thoughts, feelings, and experiences, you create a space for introspection and personal growth. This practice can help you process complex emotions, gain insights into your behavior, and articulate your goals and aspirations.

The act of writing engages both the analytical and creative parts of your brain, making journaling a comprehensive tool for self-discovery. Whether it's a gratitude journal, a diary of daily events, or a collection of personal reflections, the format can be tailored to your needs. By consistently journaling, you develop a clearer understanding of yourself and your journey, creating a record that can be revisited and reflected upon.

Journaling also offers a safe space for exploring difficult emotions and experiences. By putting your thoughts on paper, you externalize them, making them easier to confront and understand. This practice can lead to catharsis and healing, providing a sense of relief and resolution. Over time, journaling can become a cornerstone of emotional wellbeing, fostering resilience and self-awareness.

Sharing your journaling practice with others can create opportunities for connection and support. By discussing your reflections and insights, you open the door to deeper conversations and mutual understanding. Collaborative journaling, where friends or family members write together or share entries, can strengthen relationships by fostering empathy and shared experiences.

5

Chapter 5: Evening Rituals for Restful Sleep

Just as morning rituals set the tone for the day, evening rituals can pave the way for restful sleep and rejuvenation. Establishing a consistent bedtime routine helps signal to your body that it's time to wind down, promoting relaxation and improving sleep quality. Simple actions like dimming the lights, reading a book, or practicing gentle stretches can create a calming environment conducive to sleep.

Evening rituals offer an opportunity to reflect on the day's events and release any lingering stress or tension. Activities like journaling, meditating, or enjoying a warm cup of herbal tea can help quiet the mind and prepare it for rest. By intentionally slowing down and engaging in soothing practices, you create a transition from the busyness of the day to the tranquility of the night.

The benefits of evening rituals extend beyond sleep quality. A peaceful bedtime routine can enhance overall mental and emotional wellbeing by reducing stress and promoting relaxation. These habits create a sense of closure and completeness, allowing you to end the day on a positive note and wake up feeling refreshed and ready to face new challenges.

Sharing evening rituals with loved ones can foster connection and intimacy. Activities like reading together, discussing the day's highlights, or practicing bedtime yoga can create shared moments of relaxation and bonding. By prioritizing these small habits, you strengthen ties and create a sense of community and support within your household.

6

Chapter 6: The Impact of Gratitude Practices

Gratitude is a powerful emotion that can transform your outlook on life and enhance your overall wellbeing. Cultivating a daily gratitude practice helps shift your focus from what you lack to what you have, fostering a mindset of abundance and appreciation. Simple habits like writing down three things you're grateful for each day or expressing gratitude to others can create profound positive shifts in your mental and emotional state.

Gratitude practices can be integrated into various aspects of your daily routine. Morning reflections, evening journaling, or spontaneous expressions of thanks can all serve as anchors for gratitude. These small habits help you cultivate a sense of mindfulness and presence, allowing you to fully appreciate the richness of your life and the people around you.

The benefits of gratitude extend beyond personal wellbeing. Expressing gratitude to others can strengthen relationships and create a sense of connection and mutual appreciation. By acknowledging and appreciating the contributions of friends, family, and colleagues, you foster a culture of kindness and support. These interactions can deepen bonds and create a positive ripple effect within your community.

Gratitude practices have been shown to improve physical health, reduce stress, and enhance overall happiness. By consistently engaging in these habits, you create a foundation of positivity and resilience that can help you navigate life's challenges with grace and optimism. The simple act of giving thanks can transform your perspective and enrich your daily experience.

7

Chapter 7: The Benefits of Physical Movement

Physical movement is an essential aspect of overall health and wellbeing. Incorporating small habits of movement into your daily routine can have profound effects on your physical, mental, and emotional state. Activities like stretching, walking, or engaging in short bursts of exercise can serve as anchors for grounding and rejuvenation, helping you maintain focus and reduce stress.

Movement practices can be tailored to your individual needs and preferences. Whether it's a morning yoga session, a lunchtime walk, or a few minutes of stretching before bed, finding ways to move your body throughout the day can enhance your energy levels and improve your mood. These small habits create opportunities for mindfulness and presence, allowing you to connect with your body and breath.

The benefits of physical movement extend beyond immediate effects. Regular movement can improve overall physical health, enhance cognitive function, and promote emotional resilience. By integrating these habits into your daily routine, you create a foundation for long-term wellbeing and vitality. Movement becomes a form of self-care, helping you maintain balance and harmony in your life.

Sharing movement practices with others can strengthen relationships and create a sense of community. Activities like group walks, dance sessions, or fitness challenges can foster connection and mutual support. By engaging in physical movement together, you create shared experiences and reinforce bonds, enhancing both individual and collective wellbeing. Whether it's a leisurely walk through the park or an invigorating workout, moving together can be a joyful and fulfilling experience that strengthens social bonds and enhances overall quality of life.

8

Chapter 8: Digital Detox for Mental Clarity

In today's digital age, the constant barrage of information and notifications can easily overwhelm our minds. Taking regular breaks from screens and digital devices can significantly improve mental clarity and overall wellbeing. Small habits like scheduling tech-free hours, setting boundaries for screen time, and engaging in offline activities can create a healthier balance between the digital and physical worlds.

A digital detox allows your mind to rest and recharge, reducing the mental clutter that can accumulate from constant connectivity. By intentionally stepping away from screens, you give yourself the opportunity to engage in more meaningful and fulfilling activities. Whether it's reading a book, spending time outdoors, or engaging in a creative hobby, these moments of disconnect can bring a renewed sense of focus and presence.

In addition to personal benefits, digital detox practices can enhance relationships. By reducing screen time, you create more opportunities for face-to-face interactions and meaningful connections with others. Whether it's enjoying a meal without devices, having a tech-free date night, or engaging in shared activities, these moments of undivided attention can strengthen bonds and foster deeper connections.

Creating a sustainable digital detox routine involves setting realistic goals and boundaries. It's important to recognize that technology is an integral part of modern life, but finding a healthy balance is key. By incorporating regular breaks and mindful usage of digital devices, you can create a more harmonious and fulfilling relationship with technology.

9

Chapter 9: Acts of Kindness for Emotional Fulfillment

Engaging in acts of kindness, no matter how small, can have a profound impact on your emotional wellbeing. Simple gestures like complimenting a colleague, helping a neighbor, or volunteering your time can create a sense of purpose and fulfillment. These acts of kindness not only benefit others but also contribute to your own happiness and satisfaction.

The practice of kindness can be integrated into daily life through intentional habits. Setting a goal to perform one kind act each day, whether it's a random act of kindness or a planned gesture, can create a ripple effect of positivity. By focusing on the needs and wellbeing of others, you shift your perspective and cultivate a mindset of compassion and empathy.

Acts of kindness can also strengthen social connections and build a sense of community. When you extend kindness to others, you create opportunities for reciprocity and mutual support. These interactions can lead to deeper relationships and a greater sense of belonging. Kindness fosters a culture of generosity and collaboration, enhancing the overall quality of life for everyone involved.

Research has shown that engaging in acts of kindness can improve mental health, reduce stress, and increase overall happiness. By making kindness a daily habit, you create a foundation of emotional resilience and positivity.

The simple act of brightening someone's day can have lasting effects on your own sense of wellbeing and fulfillment.

10

Chapter 10: Creative Expression for Emotional Release

Creative expression is a powerful tool for emotional release and self-discovery. Engaging in activities like painting, writing, music, or dance allows you to process and express complex emotions in a healthy and constructive way. These creative outlets provide a safe space for exploring your inner world and finding meaning in your experiences.

Incorporating creative habits into your daily routine can enhance your overall mental and emotional wellbeing. Whether it's setting aside time for a creative hobby, journaling your thoughts and feelings, or experimenting with new forms of expression, these activities can bring joy and fulfillment. Creative expression allows you to tap into your imagination and connect with your authentic self.

Creative pursuits can also foster a sense of accomplishment and purpose. By setting and achieving creative goals, you build confidence and resilience. The process of creating something unique and meaningful can be incredibly rewarding, providing a sense of pride and satisfaction. These experiences contribute to a positive self-image and a greater sense of self-worth.

Sharing your creative endeavors with others can strengthen relationships and build a sense of community. Whether it's collaborating on a project, sharing your work, or participating in creative groups, these interactions create opportunities for connection and support. Creative expression becomes a shared experience that brings people together and fosters a sense of belonging.

11

Chapter 11: Mindful Communication for Stronger Connections

Mindful communication is the practice of being fully present and attentive during interactions with others. By listening actively, expressing yourself clearly, and responding with empathy, you create deeper and more meaningful connections. These habits can transform your relationships and enhance your overall social wellbeing.

Mindful communication begins with active listening. By truly hearing and understanding the perspectives of others, you create a sense of validation and respect. This practice involves focusing on the speaker, maintaining eye contact, and avoiding interruptions. By giving your full attention, you foster trust and openness in your interactions.

Expressing yourself mindfully involves clear and honest communication. By articulating your thoughts and feelings with respect and consideration, you create a positive and constructive dialogue. This practice includes using "I" statements, being mindful of your tone and body language, and seeking to understand rather than to be understood.

Responding with empathy is a key component of mindful communication. By acknowledging and validating the emotions and experiences of others, you create a supportive and compassionate environment. This practice involves putting yourself in the other person's shoes, offering encouragement, and being present in the moment.

Mindful communication can strengthen relationships and build a sense of community. By practicing these habits, you create deeper connections and foster a culture of mutual respect and understanding. These interactions contribute to a positive social environment and enhance overall quality of life.

12

Chapter 12: Decluttering for Mental Space

Physical clutter can have a significant impact on mental clarity and overall wellbeing. Taking the time to declutter your living and working spaces can create a sense of order and calm. Simple habits like organizing your belongings, setting aside time for regular cleaning, and letting go of unnecessary items can create a more peaceful and focused environment.

Decluttering begins with assessing your physical space and identifying areas that need attention. By sorting through your belongings and deciding what to keep, donate, or discard, you create a sense of control and intentionality. This process can be both practical and therapeutic, allowing you to create a space that reflects your values and priorities.

Maintaining a clutter-free environment involves creating sustainable habits. Setting aside time for regular tidying, establishing designated spaces for items, and being mindful of new acquisitions can help prevent clutter from accumulating. These practices create a sense of order and predictability, enhancing your overall sense of wellbeing.

The benefits of decluttering extend beyond physical space. A tidy environment can improve mental clarity, reduce stress, and increase productivity. By creating a space that is free of distractions, you can focus more effectively and approach tasks with a clear mind. This sense of order and simplicity can have a positive impact on your overall quality of life.

Sharing decluttering practices with others can strengthen relationships and create a sense of community. Engaging in group decluttering sessions, offering to help friends or family with their spaces, or exchanging tips and strategies can create opportunities for connection and support. These interactions contribute to a shared sense of accomplishment and wellbeing.

13

Chapter 13: Nature Connection for Grounding

Spending time in nature is a powerful way to ground yourself and reconnect with the world around you. Engaging in activities like walking in the park, gardening, or simply sitting outside can have profound effects on your mental and emotional wellbeing. These small habits create opportunities for mindfulness and presence, allowing you to connect with the natural world.

Nature connection begins with intentional time spent outdoors. Whether it's taking a leisurely stroll, enjoying a picnic, or tending to a garden, these activities create a sense of tranquility and grounding. By immersing yourself in nature, you can escape the hustle and bustle of daily life and find a sense of peace and clarity.

The benefits of nature connection extend beyond immediate relaxation. Spending time in natural environments has been shown to reduce stress, improve mood, and enhance overall mental health. These experiences create a sense of balance and harmony, fostering a deeper connection with yourself and the world around you.

Nature connection can also strengthen relationships and build a sense of community. Engaging in outdoor activities with friends or family creates opportunities for shared experiences and meaningful conversations. Whether it's hiking together, planting a garden, or simply enjoying the beauty of nature, these moments of connection can enhance social bonds and create lasting memories.

Creating a routine of nature connection involves setting aside regular time for outdoor activities. By prioritizing these habits, you can create a more balanced and fulfilling life. Nature connection becomes a source of inspiration and rejuvenation, providing a sense of grounding and perspective.

14

Chapter 14: Financial Mindfulness for Stability

Financial mindfulness is the practice of being intentional and aware of your financial decisions and habits. By creating a budget, setting financial goals, and tracking your expenses, you can create a sense of stability and control. These habits can reduce financial stress and enhance overall wellbeing.

Financial mindfulness begins with assessing your current financial situation. By taking an honest look at your income, expenses, and savings, you can create a clear picture of your financial health. This process involves setting realistic goals, identifying areas for improvement, and creating a plan for achieving financial stability.

Maintaining financial mindfulness involves creating sustainable habits. Setting aside time for regular financial check-ins, tracking your spending, and adjusting your budget as needed can help you stay on track. These practices create a sense of accountability and intentionality, enhancing your overall sense of control and security.

The benefits of financial mindfulness extend beyond financial stability. By reducing financial stress, you can improve your overall mental and emotional wellbeing. These habits create a sense of confidence and empowerment, allowing you to approach financial decisions with clarity and purpose.

Financial mindfulness can also strengthen relationships and build a sense of community. By discussing financial goals and strategies with loved ones, you create opportunities for support and collaboration. These interactions contribute to a shared sense of accomplishment and wellbeing, enhancing overall quality of life.

15

Chapter 15: Mindful Consumption for Sustainability

Mindful consumption is the practice of being intentional and conscious about the products and services you use. By considering the environmental and social impacts of your choices, you can contribute to a more sustainable and equitable world. Simple habits like reducing waste, supporting ethical brands, and making informed purchasing decisions can create a positive ripple effect on the planet and society.

Mindful consumption begins with awareness. By educating yourself about the sources and production methods of the items you use, you can make more informed choices. This practice involves researching brands, reading labels, and considering the lifecycle of products. By choosing items that align with your values, you can support sustainable and ethical practices.

Reducing waste is a key component of mindful consumption. Small habits like recycling, composting, and minimizing single-use plastics can significantly reduce your environmental footprint. By reusing and repurposing items, you create a more sustainable lifestyle and contribute to the conservation of natural resources. These practices create a sense of responsibility and stewardship for the planet.

Supporting ethical brands and businesses can also have a positive impact.

By prioritizing companies that adhere to fair labor practices, environmentally friendly production methods, and social responsibility, you contribute to a more equitable and sustainable economy. These choices create a demand for ethical products and encourage businesses to adopt more sustainable practices.

Mindful consumption can strengthen relationships and build a sense of community. By discussing sustainable practices with friends and family, you create opportunities for shared learning and collaboration. These interactions contribute to a culture of awareness and responsibility, enhancing overall quality of life for everyone involved.

16

Chapter 16: Meditation for Mental Clarity

Meditation is a powerful tool for achieving mental clarity and emotional balance. By dedicating time each day to quiet the mind and focus on the present moment, you can reduce stress, improve concentration, and enhance overall wellbeing. Simple meditation practices like deep breathing, visualization, and mindfulness can create a sense of calm and clarity.

Meditation begins with finding a quiet space and setting aside a few minutes each day for practice. By focusing on your breath or a specific mantra, you create a sense of presence and mindfulness. This practice helps quiet the mind and reduce the constant chatter of thoughts, allowing you to experience a deeper sense of peace and clarity.

Regular meditation practice can lead to cumulative benefits. Over time, you may find that you can approach challenges with greater calm and resilience. Meditation helps improve emotional regulation, enhance self-awareness, and foster a greater sense of inner peace. These habits create a foundation for long-term mental and emotional wellbeing.

Sharing meditation practices with others can strengthen relationships and build a sense of community. Group meditation sessions, mindfulness classes, or simply meditating with a friend can create opportunities for connection and support. These shared experiences enhance social bonds and contribute to a positive and peaceful environment.

17

Chapter 17: The Journey of Personal Growth

Personal growth is a lifelong journey of self-discovery, learning, and transformation. By embracing small habits and practices that foster growth, you can create a more fulfilling and meaningful life. Reflecting on your experiences, setting goals, and seeking new opportunities for learning and development can enhance your overall sense of purpose and fulfillment.

The journey of personal growth begins with self-awareness. By taking the time to reflect on your strengths, weaknesses, and aspirations, you create a foundation for intentional living. This practice involves setting realistic and achievable goals, identifying areas for improvement, and celebrating your accomplishments. By being honest with yourself and embracing a growth mindset, you can navigate life's challenges with resilience and grace.

Seeking new opportunities for learning and development is a key component of personal growth. Whether it's pursuing a new hobby, taking a class, or seeking mentorship, these experiences can broaden your horizons and enhance your skills. By staying curious and open to new possibilities, you create a dynamic and enriching life.

Personal growth can also strengthen relationships and build a sense of community. By sharing your journey with others, you create opportunities

CHAPTER 17: THE JOURNEY OF PERSONAL GROWTH

for mutual support and encouragement. These interactions foster a culture of growth and collaboration, enhancing overall quality of life for everyone involved.

As you continue on your journey of personal growth, remember that it is a continuous and evolving process. Embrace each moment as an opportunity for learning and transformation. By cultivating small habits and practices that align with your values and aspirations, you can create a life that is grounded, fulfilling, and deeply meaningful.

In the end, these daily anchors—morning rituals, breathing techniques, mindful eating, journaling, evening rituals, gratitude practices, physical movement, digital detox, acts of kindness, creative expression, mindful communication, decluttering, nature connection, financial mindfulness, mindful consumption, meditation, and personal growth—serve as the cornerstones for a balanced and enriching life. By integrating these small habits into your daily routine, you create a foundation of focus, calm, and connection that can carry you through life's journey. May you find strength, clarity, and joy in these practices, and may they guide you toward a life that is grounded and deeply fulfilling.

In a world filled with constant noise and distractions, finding moments of peace and connection can feel like an elusive quest. "**Daily Anchors: Small Habits to Ground Your Focus, Calm Your Mind, and Strengthen Ties**" offers a refreshing guide to cultivating habits that bring balance and meaning to your daily life.

This book explores the transformative power of small, intentional practices that can ground your focus, calm your mind, and strengthen your ties with others. Each of the 17 chapters delves into a specific habit, from morning rituals to mindful eating, breathing techniques to acts of kindness. With four elaborate paragraphs in each chapter, you'll discover practical tips and heartfelt insights to integrate these habits into your routine.

Learn how to create a serene morning routine that sets the tone for a productive day, practice breathing techniques to manage stress, and embrace mindful eating to enhance your focus and presence. Discover the art of journaling for self-reflection, the benefits of evening rituals for restful sleep, and the impact of gratitude practices on your overall well-being.

Through engaging narratives and actionable advice, "Daily Anchors" inspires you to build a foundation of small habits that lead to profound personal growth and stronger relationships. Whether you're seeking mental clarity, emotional balance, or deeper connections with loved ones, this book offers a roadmap to a more grounded, fulfilling life.

www.ingramcontent.com/pod-product-compliance
Lightning Source LLC
LaVergne TN
LVHW010441070526
838199LV00066B/6123